A souvenir guide

# Thomas Hardy's Homes

## Dorset

**National Trust**

# Foreword

A visit to the cottage at Bockhampton is an emotional experience for anyone who loves Hardy's work. The place brims with meaning, because his imagination was shaped by the landscape of his childhood. The novels and poems arose from what he saw then — cottage, meadow, heath, hill, woodland. Also from what he heard. His grandmother told him stories of the past, and as a boy he walked with his father to villages round about, each carrying his fiddle, to make music for parties and weddings. He knew the roads, the farms, the churches and churchyards, and the people. If the novels are unconsoling, showing country life as harsh and tragic, at the same time they, and the poems, celebrate the beauty and strangeness of the natural world as he had absorbed it.

Growing up he was attracted to London and lived there for long spells, but he was always drawn back to his native Dorset, and in the 1880s he planned and built Max Gate, within walking distance of Bockhampton. It is an awkward house, but one that suited him, and it remained his home for the rest of his life.

He used the old name 'Wessex' for the first time in *Far From the Madding Crowd* for what he called a 'partly real, partly dream-country'. The ambiguity was fruitful for him and for his readers. He mixed real place names with invented ones in the maps he drew for each new

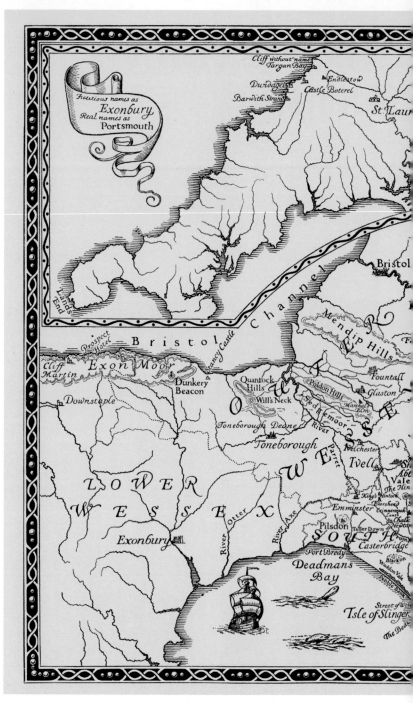

Left The Wessex of Thomas Hardy's Novels and Poems, based on Bertram Windle's 1902 map, created in collaboration with the author

book, and public interest grew. Letters came from readers wanting to settle in 'Wessex', and in 1912 he suggested to his publishers that his complete novels should be marketed in a Wessex edition. The next year his friend Hermann Lea published *Thomas Hardy's Wessex*, a guide with photographs, with Hardy's blessing.

With his growing fame came troops of visitors to Max Gate. Mrs Patrick Campbell came, and Hardy played his fiddle for her to dance. Yeats arrived to give him a gold medal and was entertained by Emma Hardy's cats sitting beside him on the dining table. The Prince of Wales was sent to lunch with the great writer he had not actually read. Gustav Holst came, seeking permission to dedicate his tone poem 'Egdon Heath' to him. Robert Graves, Walter de la Mare and Siegfried Sassoon all paid their warm respects to the master. Virginia and Leonard Woolf made the train journey from London, four hours each way, to take tea, and were both impressed: he offered Leonard whisky and confided to Virginia his preference for solitude over rounds of visitors.

His novels had been greeted with condescension by many, found shocking and morally subversive by some, and warmly admired by others for their truthfulness and bold rejection of conventional thinking. He gave up writing novels but wrote poetry to the last day of his life. Time has brought ever more admirers, and today in the 21st century men and women come from every part of the world to walk in his footsteps and to breathe the inspiring air of Bockhampton and Max Gate. Anna Groves's *Thomas Hardy's Homes* is a welcome guide for all such visitors.

Claire Tomalin
Author of *Thomas Hardy: The Time-Torn Man*

# Thomas Hardy's Homes

A thatched cottage and a red-brick villa: in one a great writer was born; in the other he died, recalling memories of his childhood home. In these two houses he gained his inspiration and composed his detailed observations of the world, sometimes suffused with light, at other times darkly despairing.

On 2 June 1840, in a three-roomed cottage on Cherry Lane, Higher Bockhampton, a son was born to Thomas and Jemima Hardy, their first child. Infant mortality rates at that time were high (about one in six) and when the baby boy came into the world silent and still, it was assumed the couple had been unlucky. However, the midwife saw that he was alive. Although he continued to be a delicate child, Thomas Hardy lived a long life and published 14 novels, nearly a thousand poems and 49 short stories. He died, aged 87, at home at Max Gate in Dorchester, just three miles from the place of his birth.

## A cautionary note

Thomas loved objects for their comforting familiarity rather than their material value. 'The beauty of association,' he wrote, 'is entirely superior to the beauty of aspect, and a beloved relative's old battered tankard to the finest Greek vase.' Although when left to the National Trust both houses were unfurnished, it is this homeliness of the 'relative's old

Below left A view of the cottage from the heath by Thomas's first wife Emma

Below right Hardy and his mother

Opposite The porch at Max Gate

battered tankard' that we have attempted to recreate in Hardy's homes.

On the death of Hardy's second wife, Florence, in 1937, Max Gate and most of its contents were sold at auction. Under Florence's will a number of books from the library, letters, manuscripts and the contents of Hardy's study were left to the Dorset County Museum where there is a permanent display of Hardy treasures and a reconstruction of his study. Fortunately for us, Thomas's sister, Kate, bought Max Gate, and on her death in 1940 left it to the National Trust. She also left a bequest for the purchase of the cottage when possible; this came to fruition in 1948.

So Thomas Hardy's homes contain few of his possessions, but what they retain is atmosphere, a sense of the people who lived there, the passing of time, and the cycle of the seasons. So it is perhaps appropriate not to focus on material things but to enjoy the atmosphere of these places as Thomas would have known them.

## Different homes

Thomas enjoyed atmosphere and landscape, most obviously that of his childhood home. At the cottage it is easy to imagine the scenes depicted in his early novels. His childhood appears to have been generally happy and it was to this home that Thomas returned during his early manhood, leaving it only when he married.

Life at Max Gate, where he lived for the last 42 years of his life, seems to have been less happy. Here his later works, darker in nature and tone, were written, and his literary career went from strength to strength. Many distinguished visitors came to pay court to the great writer.

But his heart truly belonged to the place of his birth; when Hardy took to his bed in Max Gate for the last time, his thoughts were of the cottage in Bockhampton, his last wish being to smell bacon cooked over the fire, in the way his mother used to do it.

# Thomas Hardy's roots

**All his life Thomas Hardy was keenly aware of class. In the rigidly structured system of Victorian rural society, the Hardys would have known their place. Although Hardy always liked to claim kinship with various famous Hardys of Dorset, his immediate family connections were modest. They were relatively well-off, self-employed smallholders, renting their land from the Kingston Maurward estate, but able to build and extend their home as the family grew.**

The cottage at Bockhampton was built in 1800 by the writer's great-grandfather John Hardy, a mason who established his own business, for his son Thomas (the First), who followed him into the family business. Thomas was a keen musician, playing bass viol (cello) for Stinsford Church, and by 1830 he was regularly accompanied by two of his sons on violin. One of these sons was Thomas (the Second) who, in his turn, took over the business and cottage. He was also musical and had a keen interest in folklore. He married Jemima Hand, who had experienced a more difficult childhood and whose family had come down in the world. She had gone into service at the age of 13, but was fortunate to find work with employers like

Above Hardy's father, Thomas Hardy (the Second), and Hardy's mother, Jemima

Opposite Hardy aged 16, when he was an architect's apprentice

Below Hardy's father's tune book

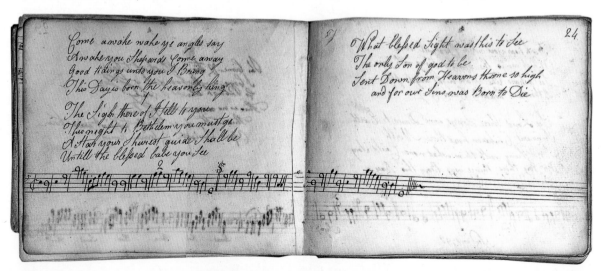

Reverend Charles Fox-Strangways, a scholar and a cleric, who recognised her enthusiasm for learning and encouraged her reading.

Their child, Thomas the Third, who became the great writer, was very much a product of his upbringing and the world around him. His novels and short stories are set in the fictional region of Wessex. They portray a range of vivid characters caught up in compelling stories, and explore the themes of love, class and the natural world, amongst others. His work also shows a deep awareness of the inequalities and rigidity of Victorian society, as well as the realities of rural life and the ways in which it was changing.

With his mother's ambitions behind him, and his poor health from childhood hampering him physically, Thomas Hardy was not destined for the family business. Jemima ensured he had the best education they could provide; at 16 he was apprenticed to John Hicks, a local architect, with whom his father worked and who, having seen Thomas assist at a survey, said he would like to take him on as a pupil. Thomas thus moved up a social step by entering a profession and it was one for which his familiarity with the building trade and his artistic talents particularly fitted him. Sketching had long been a favourite pastime for Thomas and his early drawings show the potential for meticulous draughtsmanship.

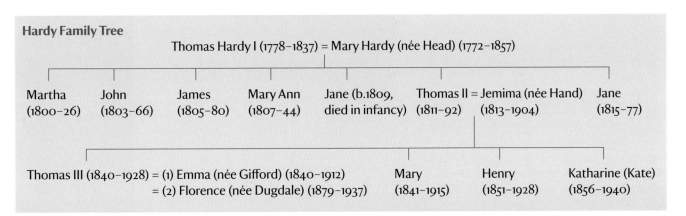

## Hardy Family Tree

Thomas Hardy I (1778–1837) = Mary Hardy (née Head) (1772–1857)

| Martha (1800–26) | John (1803–66) | James (1805–80) | Mary Ann (1807–44) | Jane (b.1809, died in infancy) | Thomas II (1811–92) = Jemima (née Hand) (1813–1904) | Jane (1815–77) |

Thomas III (1840–1928) = (1) Emma (née Gifford) (1840–1912)
= (2) Florence (née Dugdale) (1879–1937)

Mary (1841–1915)

Henry (1851–1928)

Katharine (Kate) (1856–1940)

# The Hardys' Rural Life

The cottage where Thomas Hardy was born, with its overhanging thatch and uneven windows, and with roses, japonica and honeysuckle climbing the walls, has an appearance which captures the imagination. Generations later, it is still possible to imagine the life Hardy and his family lived here and to experience the atmosphere that inspired him.

At the time the cottage was built, it would have occupied an isolated spot on the edge of the heath, three miles north-east of Dorchester. It was built from cob – a mix of clay with local materials, such as gravel, sand, chalk or flint, dug from the surrounding area and bound together with straw, then combined with water – plastered with lime from the family's limekiln, and thatched with wheat straw and local hazel from coppice. The front was faced in brick to protect the cob from the elements.

The original building consisted of a family room and two bedrooms. It has thick walls, squared and chamfered beams, and chestnut floorboards. The extension was built with less care and more speed, with thinner walls and larch or deal for the floors. You can see the later additions by looking at the roof from the garden, the lower line of the thatch showing the division.

The original cottage was where Thomas the First, his wife Mary and their children lived. Thomas the Second (1811–92) then lived here with Jemima (1814–1904) and their four children, two boys and two girls, of whom our Thomas was the eldest. The extension was where Mary lived after her husband's death, and both extension and the family cottage

had their own front doors. You can clearly see, to the left and right of the porch, the blocked doorways filled in with rubble that were once the separate entrances. Less obvious, but captured beautifully in one of Thomas Hardy's poems, are the worn flagstones in the Parlour indicating where people once entered the cottage (see page 11). After Granny died, the cottage was altered to include her rooms.

Thomas was the eldest of four children born between 1840 and 1856. Before Granny's death in 1857 there would have been seven people living in the cottage. It was a rustic beginning for this great writer. Granny was a skilled storyteller; Thomas's mother was a great reader; his father was a musician and a lover of nature. Thomas observed his family and the friends who came to dances, choir practices, christenings and picnics. He later absorbed these influences and people into his stories and he used the natural life around him to complement the human scene.

Opposite This view of the cottage shows the different levels in the roof; the right-hand section was a later addition

# The Parlour

Left of the porch is the Parlour, the heart and hearth of the Hardy home. The fuel for the fire was collected from the woods and heath behind the cottage. In this room the family would prepare their food, boil the kettle for tea and socialise by the deep inglenook. A copper would have heated water for laundry, washing and cooking.

The warmth from this relatively large, social room would have helped heat the bedrooms above. A staircase once led from this room to where the family slept upstairs, but when the cottages were combined the stairs were moved to the room next door. The deep west-facing window-seats and leaded lights give the appearance of a much older building, but the Hardys were rural builders and used old-fashioned methods.

Above The welcoming fireplace in the Parlour was the scene of many a convivial gathering

## The family that plays together

The Hardy men were very musical. Thomas's father played the bass viol and Thomas and his brother Henry both played the violin. In the Parlour you will see the sorts of instruments they used. Thomas cherished the family instruments he inherited, and proudly displayed his violin alongside his father's violin and grandfather's cello in his study at Max Gate. Some of these can now be seen in the Dorset County Museum.

*Silent Christmas Voices.*

*The Study, Max Gate (Fiddle Corner)*

In addition to the relocated staircase, the front door was moved and a window was added here. The worn flagstones below the right-hand window give this away and gave Hardy inspiration in the poem 'The Self-Unseeing'.

> *Here is the ancient floor,*
> *Footworn and hollowed and thin,*
> *Here was the former door*
> *Where the dead feet walked in.*
>
> *She sat here in her chair,*
> *Smiling into the fire;*
> *He who played stood there,*
> *Bowing it higher and higher.*
>
> *Childlike, I danced in a dream;*
> *Blessings emblazoned that day;*
> *Everything glowed with a gleam;*
> *Yet we were looking away!*

Right The window in the Parlour used to be a doorway – you can glimpse the worn flagstones beneath

This poem testifies to the many family celebrations that this room would have seen. The large Portland flagstones, worn in places, bear witness to the passage of feet and the kicking up of heels. Reading the description of the Christmas party in *Under the Greenwood Tree*, in which seven couples perform a dance called 'The Triumph' in the Dewys' parlour, it is possible to imagine just such a scene in this room.

# The Office

This was the scullery of the original cottage, but was later used by Hardy's father as his office. Here the accounts were managed and the workers were paid, through the small window looking out on to Cherry Lane and the heath beyond.

Thomas's father was a stonemason, but in the 1851 census, he is described as a 'bricklayer' with two employees. By 1871 this had risen to eight men, plus a boy. When Thomas's brother Henry took over the family business, it prospered further.

## Destined for greater things

Thomas's mother, Jemima, was keen to encourage her elder son's education and he was sent first to Mrs Martin's village school a mile away in Lower Bockhampton, and then to Isaac Last's in Dorchester, where he started to learn Latin and where he read widely. At the age of 16 Hardy was apprenticed to local architect John Hicks, where he applied himself to his studies but also developed interests in many other fields, including classical Greek.

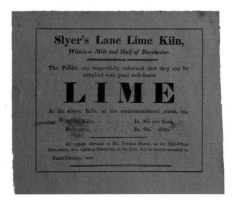

Left **Lime advert**
Below left **Hardy aged 19**
Opposite **Cottage window through which labourers were paid**

The poet William Barnes ran a school next door to Hicks's office and he became an important mentor to Thomas, who often went to question him about academic matters.

Another great influence was Horace Moule, son of Henry Moule, vicar of Fordington and inventor of the dry earth closet (see page 21). Exceptionally intelligent and charismatic, Horace was the sort of sophisticated, educated man Thomas aspired to be. However, Horace was as troubled as he was brilliant; he turned in his anguish to opium and alcohol, and died by his own hand, in September 1873 aged 41. That was the year before Hardy published *Far From the Madding Crowd*, his fourth novel, which was so successful that it gave him the financial security to marry. He had met his first wife, Emma, in 1870 and she too had a powerful influence on Hardy. It was she who encouraged him to give up architecture and dedicate himself to writing.

### The Hardy brothers

Thomas and Henry were born 11 years apart and were quite different personalities, but they always enjoyed a good relationship. They took several trips together including cycling tours of Dorset and visits to Lincoln, Ely, Cambridge and Canterbury. Henry was once engaged but never married.

# The Sisters' Bedroom

**This is where Thomas's sisters would have slept. Through the idiosyncratically angled windows you can peer under the 'eyebrows' of the thatched roof to enjoy views of the Garden and Orchard.**

Although known as the Sisters' Bedroom, with Mary born a year after Thomas in 1841 and Kate born in 1856, they wouldn't have shared it for long before Mary went to teacher training college in 1860.

## Jobs for the girls

Jemima did not want any of her children to marry, and Thomas was the only one who did. She wanted her daughters to have independent means so that marriage was not a necessity for them. Both were thoroughly educated. When Mary was 18, Thomas escorted her to teacher training college at Salisbury. He drew on her experience there in two of his novels. In *Under*

*the Greenwood Tree,* Fancy Day is sent to teacher training college so that 'if any gentleman … should want to marry her, and she want to marry him, he shan't be her superior in pocket.' The training Mary received culminated in her being granted the position of headmistress at the Bell Street National School in Dorchester.

Kate, too, trained as a teacher and after her first teaching post at Sandford Orcas near Sherborne, she returned to the Dorchester area. She then lived with her sister until Mary's death in 1915, first in a house bought for them by Thomas, and later at 'Talbothays', which he had built for them and their brother Henry.

Above **The Sisters' Bedroom**

Left **Mary Hardy as a girl**

Far left **Kate Hardy as a young lady**

# The Parents' Bedroom

**This unremarkable room, simply furnished and with whitewashed walls, was where Thomas Hardy came into the world with barely a whimper. He was put to one side, his mother seen to and consoled, but then the midwife discerned signs of life.**

This room is the scene of Thomas's earliest memory, one that is evoked by the cot in the corner. In the cottage Thomas grew up close to nature, on the edge of the heath and woodland. However, on one occasion, he was closer to nature than most parents would like. One hot afternoon his mother came into the house to find Thomas asleep in his cradle with a large snake curled up on his chest, also sleeping peacefully. Throughout his life, Thomas maintained an affinity with animals and later he used his fame to speak out against cruelty to them.

## Supportive in their different ways

While Jemima was perhaps the stricter parent, Thomas enjoyed her sense of humour and love of adventure. His father was also companionable. He taught his son to play the violin and they played at weddings and parties, after which they would sometimes walk home together in the middle of the night. In the school holidays Thomas would go with his father to visit building sites and listen to him discussing the work with the architect. In the autumn they would gather apples together. When Thomas senior died in 1901 Hardy wrote the poem 'Bereft' (see also 'To My Father's Violin'). Jemima was 90 years old when she died three years later and she too was greatly mourned by her son (see the poem 'After the Last Breath').

Right **The Parents' Bedroom with the cot in the corner**

# Thomas's Bedroom

**The narrow passage leading to this room was made when the cottages were knocked through, and shows the thickness of the outer wall with its chimneybreast. This was where Granny once slept. Some time after her death in 1857 this became Thomas's bedroom, later shared with his little brother Henry, born in 1851.**

This wasn't a long-term arrangement as Thomas left for London in 1862. He found employment with Arthur Blomfield, one of the most successful architects of the time, and was earning a respectable wage, much of which he spent on visiting museums and galleries, and attending plays and operas. Immersed in the cultural life of the capital, he was writing in earnest, especially poems.

However in 1867 the breakdown of a relationship and ill-health – the result of too many hours of reading, too little sleep and exercise, plus the unhealthy atmosphere of London – caused Hardy's work at the office to suffer. A timely request from John Hicks, his previous employer in Dorchester, for an assistant, led to his returning to Bockhampton. Working for Hicks allowed Hardy plenty of time for serious writing. The table under the window is a replica of the one at which Thomas Hardy wrote some of his early novels. The original can be seen in the Dorset County Museum.

## A shaky start

After Hardy's return to Dorset he wrote *The Poor Man and the Lady,* his first novel. The rigid nature of Victorian society is a recurrent theme in Hardy's novels and short stories. The romance between people of different social classes implied by the title of this first novel did not fit what was acceptable and the novel was therefore never published. It no longer exists in its complete form but Hardy used aspects of it in later works.

Above Thomas's Bedroom window; it was here that Hardy wrote his early novels

Right Hardy in his thirties

Below The title pages of Hardy's first three published novels. Notice how the third book, *A Pair of Blue Eyes*, clearly states Hardy as the author – his first two books were published anonymously

Despite this rejection, the publishers Hardy approached encouraged him to continue writing. In particular, the novelist George Meredith, the reader for Chapman and Hall, whom Hardy met in 1869, advised him to aim for a stronger plot rather than social comment. This was advice which was clearly taken in Hardy's first published novel,

*Desperate Remedies*. William Tinsley, who published it, also accepted his next manuscript, *Under the Greenwood Tree*. This is a novel with vivid descriptions of rural life and scenes that can only have been inspired by this cottage on the edge of the heath. It was received well; Thomas had found where his best inspiration lay. His next novel, *A Pair of Blue Eyes*, was the work of a novelist growing in confidence and also of a man in love, as it was written during the time of his courtship of Emma Lavinia Gifford. Part of it was written in Cornwall, where he met Emma, and part of it was written here at Bockhampton.

## Family connections

When sitting at the desk looking west, Thomas would have had sight of Admiral Hardy's Monument, ten miles away on Blackdown Hill. A number of Hardy's characters harbour social pretensions, most notably Jack Durbeyfield, the father of Tess, the heroine of one of his best-loved novels. Durbeyfield believed his family to be descended from the d'Urbervilles, a noble Norman family. It is interesting to think of Hardy dreaming about a connection to the celebrated Hardys of Portesham, one of whom was another Thomas Hardy, captain of HMS *Victory* at Trafalgar, and famously present at Nelson's side to receive his last words – 'Kiss Me, Hardy'.

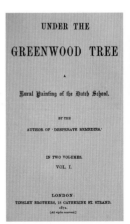

# Granny's Kitchen

**Hardy's paternal grandmother, Mary, was an influential figure in Thomas's life. She is mentioned in his poem 'Domicilium'. She not only encouraged Thomas with his reading but she would relate tales of an older Dorset than the one Thomas knew. It is this Dorset of the early 19th century that Hardy sought to capture in his writing. Nostalgia and concern for a fast-disappearing way of life are prominent in many of his novels.**

After the unexpected death of Hardy's grandfather in 1837, Mary continued to manage the accounts and remained an important figure in the household. She was evidently a rather spry old lady, judging by the steep staircase next door that leads to what was once her bedroom.

Granny's large range has been removed but a bread oven remains to its right. Fired by gorse (or 'furze' as it is still known in the

West Country and described in 'Domicilium') which was collected from the heath behind the cottage, as many as 14 loaves could be baked here at a time, and many other things such as cakes, pies and milk puddings. The long-handled wooden shovel is a peel, or pele, and was used to place items to be baked on the floor of the oven.

The kitchen would have been Mary's living-room as well as where she prepared meals, but after her death in 1857 the family used it as their kitchen, changing the access to the bread oven, which had formerly been from the Parlour, to here. From the outside you can see where Granny's front door was blocked up and made into a window.

## Excerpt from 'One We Knew'

*With cap-framed face and long gaze into the embers –*
*    We seated around her knees –*
*She would dwell on such dead themes, not as one who remembers,*
*    But rather as one who sees.*

Above right **The bread oven**

Right **The peel, or pele, propped in a corner of the Kitchen**

### Inspiring figures

Granny was born in the Berkshire village of Fawley (the surname of Jude in *Jude the Obscure*). She is possibly the inspiration for the grandmother in *Two on a Tower*. Granny was a great storyteller and the young Thomas was an avid listener. She could remember hearing the news of Marie Antoinette's execution in 1793. With a clear fondness and talent for finely drawn-out detail that was inherited by Thomas, she even recalled the pattern of the muslin dress she was ironing at the time. She lived through the Napoleonic Wars (1803–15) and her memories of a Dorset under the threat of invasion by the French clearly inspired her grandson. Hardy was always fascinated by the Napoleonic Wars. These were the subject of his epic drama, *The Dynasts*.

# The Garden and Orchard

Thomas's poem 'Domicilium' describes 'honeysucks' climbing near the door and roses in abundance; both can be seen and their scents savoured today. The Orchard, too, is a place where it is easy to imagine Thomas helping his father gather apples for cider.

The house stands in an acre of ground. The Hardys grew fruit, vegetables and herbs in the courtyard in front of the cottage, kept a pig and hens, and had a few beehives in the Orchard, all of which made the family quite self-sufficient. The well, also in front of the cottage, was a rather unusual luxury for the time; the other villagers would have had to collect their water from a communal well down the lane.

After the family left the cottage in 1912, Hardy helped the next tenant, his close friend Hermann Lea, to redesign the Garden into the quaint cottage garden you now see. Hardy's sister later wrote about their father's straight rows of vegetables, although the structure of the flower garden is Lea's addition. In the flower garden there is still some formality – the tiles edging the centre bed are said to be those from the roof of a lean-to on the original cottage –

### A great benefactor

This earth closet is an example of the form that typified Dorset cottages from the mid-19th century. Waste gathered in a pit under the seat and composted down to then be dug and used on the garden, fertilizing the vegetables. However, it also came with problems, and cases of waste leaking or overflowing from the pits were not uncommon. This led to contamination of water supplies and disease, such as typhoid, diptheria and cholera. The local Revd Henry Moule, vicar of Fordington, was horrified by the conditions that caused cholera outbreaks in Fordington. He wrote public letters to Prince Albert, campaigning for change, and in the year of the Great Stink in London (1858), he invented the dry earth closet. This simple toilet collected waste in a bucket, releasing dry earth over it from a hopper to reduce smell, and allowing the waste to be disposed of elsewhere. It was so successful in reducing disease that it was exported all over the world, solving through simplicity an age-old problem. Moule was also father to Hardy's mentor and close friend, Horace Moule, and both supported him through his early career.

Above A path in the front garden, edged with day lilies, daisies and buddleias

Opposite above The cottage, showing the vegetable garden in the foreground

Opposite below Hollyhocks in the vegetable garden, monkshood, buddleia with peacock butterfly

but the planting is otherwise informal with many classic cottage garden stalwarts such as hollyhocks, foxgloves, monkshood, cornflower, rosemary and lavender. Everlasting sweet pea grows wherever it can.

In the Orchard the Hardys grew local apples, such as Gascoyne Scarlets, Golden Pippins and Bockhampton Sweets. Today it is planted with traditional apple varieties and a medlar, a fruit once popular in this country but now fallen out of fashion. It is said that Thomas used to pick Bockhampton Sweets from the Orchard and give them to a bookseller's son in Dorchester so that he would be allowed to read the books in the shop. He also helped annually with his father's cider-making.

# Thorncombe Wood

**Thorncombe Wood to the south of the cottage was once a wild place, only navigable by those who knew it well. Now managed by Dorset County Council, it is here for all to enjoy at all times of year. Spring and early summer are a particular delight, when violets and primroses are followed by stands of foxgloves in a carpet of bluebells.**

In *The Life and Works of Thomas Hardy*, Hardy's autobiography published under his second wife's name after his death, we are told that when he was writing *Far From the Madding Crowd*, if an idea came while he was walking in the woods, he would write on 'large dead leaves, with chips left by the wood-cutters, or pieces of stone or slate that came to hand'. Whether this is to be believed, it clearly makes the point that Thomas was very much of the place of his birth and its surroundings.

## The heath that was

The heathland lay to the east and in 1840 covered about 50,000 hectares (123,500 acres). It is now under the management of the Forestry Commission. This was Thomas's fictional Egdon Heath. If you want to imagine how it must have looked in his time, the first chapter of *The Return of the Native* captures the scene, with its description of a 'heathy, furzy, briary wilderness', crossed by ancients, Saxon settlers and Roman centurions.

Above Thorncombe Wood is home to Rushy Pond and Black Heath which inspired some of Hardy's most loved work

## Cornish Romance

While working as a church architect for G. R. Crickmay in Weymouth, Hardy was sent to Cornwall in March 1870 to make plans for a restoration project on the church of St Juliot, near Boscastle. Arrangements were made for him to stay at the rectory, where he was met at the door by 'a young lady in brown', the rector's sister-in-law, Emma Lavinia Gifford. This was 7 March, a date to which, after Emma's death, Hardy's desk calendar was always set – and still is, in the reconstructed study at Dorset County Museum. A romantic relationship developed on that first visit. Hardy returned to Dorset with magic in his eyes, as related in the poem 'When I set out for Lyonnesse'. Emma was charming and high-spirited and in her own way a part of her environment – like Thomas. She rode her pony confidently along the north Cornish clifftops, her cheeks flushed and her hair floating freely in the wind. Emma had literary aspirations of her own and was surely in his mind when he

Right Portrait of Emma in her twenties

Far right Hardy's famous poem, 'When I set out for Lyonnesse', in his own hand

described Elfride Swancourt, his heroine in *A Pair of Blue Eyes*. At the beginning of their relationship Hardy and Emma would discuss his work and for many years she assisted Hardy, including writing to his dictation when he was ill for several months whilst working on *The Laodicean*.

Neither family approved of the match and the courtship was a drawn-out, long-distance one, with many months of each year apart. Nevertheless, four years after their first meeting, and with Hardy's fourth novel, *Far From the Madding Crowd*, serialised in the country's most widely read literary journal, *The Cornhill Magazine*, he had the financial security to marry Emma.

# From Hardy's Cottage to Max Gate

Every school day from 1850 to 1856 and when he was working for John Hicks, Thomas would walk the three miles to Dorchester and back again. You can walk a similar route across fields, from the cottage where Thomas Hardy was humbly born to the house where he rose to literary pre-eminence.

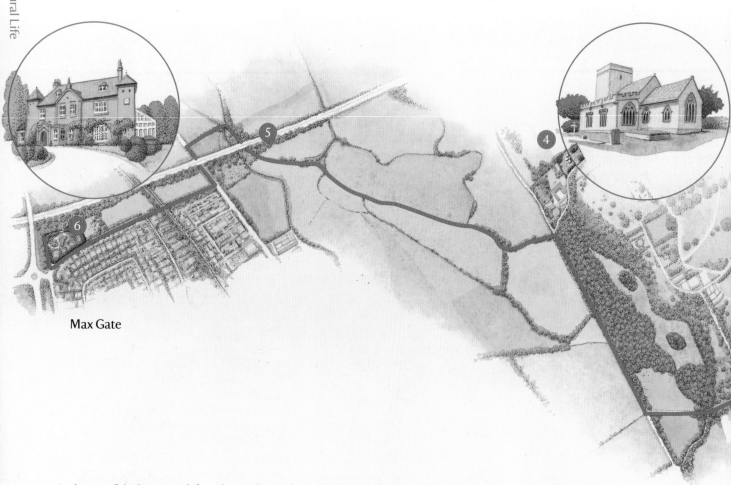

Max Gate

At the top of the lane, turn left and cross the road to turn right onto a footpath running diagonally over a field (The Drong) before meeting the road again. Cross the road and follow the footpath (slightly to your left) that continues across fields towards Kingston Maurward (the big white house).

As you come into the equine centre, bear right and pass the front of the old Elizabethan manor. Bear left round the side of it and then right, heading downhill to the weir and river. Cross the river and turn right along the river path. Keep going until you see Church Lane on your right. You can follow

Thomas would walk in all seasons and weathers, across the fields, through the woods, passing the church where his grandfather, father and uncle had played, over the water meadows, observing and communing with nature. In doing so he moved between two very different societies and environments. When he finally returned to live permanently in this part of Dorset, Dorchester was the place he chose, but when he built his own house, from the rear it looked towards Bockhampton.

'He walked along towards home without attending to paths. If anyone knew the heath well it was Clym. He was permeated with its scenes, with its substance, and with its odours. He might be said to be its product.'

From *The Return of the Native*

*this up to Stinsford Church or turn left to Dorchester (signposted). Follow the path across the watermeadows. You will pass under the A35. Follow the path to your left to St Georges Road. Turn left (back under the A35) and turn right down the green lane that runs up the side of the field*

*(before the houses). Follow this in a straight line and continue following the fields along the road. When the fields end, you will see the brick garden wall of Max Gate on your right.*

1  Hardy's Cottage
2  Thorncombe Wood
3  Cuckoo Lane
4  Stinsford Church
5  A35
6  Max Gate

# Hardy in Dorchester

If *The Return of the Native* was inspired by Egdon Heath, Casterbridge, with its infamous mayor, is undeniably Dorchester. Max Gate in Dorchester is the house that Hardy designed, where he wrote some of his finest novels, and where he became a great poet.

After their marriage in September 1874, Thomas and Emma rented a series of houses in London, Somerset and Dorset. They had two quite settled and idyllically happy years (see the poem, 'The Two-Years Idyll') in Sturminster Newton, where Thomas wrote *The Return of the Native*.

In 1883 Hardy purchased a one-and-a-half acre plot of land, to the south east of Dorchester, from the Duchy of Cornwall, for £450. While the house which Hardy designed and which came to be called Max Gate was being built, Hardy and Emma rented Shire-Hall Place in the centre of Dorchester. There Hardy wrote *The Mayor of Casterbridge*. In 1885, they moved for the last time, to Max Gate. It was here that Hardy corrected the proofs of *The Mayor of Casterbridge* and wrote

*The Woodlanders* and then *Tess of the d'Urbervilles*, a great tragic novel but one which incensed many at the time with its sympathetic portrayal of a 'fallen woman'. His final novel, *Jude the Obscure*, was met with an even stronger negative reaction, because of its criticism of marriage and its inclusion of child suicide.

Max Gate was where Hardy ended his career as a novelist and devoted himself instead to poetry, his first love. From his first unpublished novel that challenged the class system, through the tales of love and loss in the Wessex landscape, to his later works tackling contemporary attitudes to sex and religion, Thomas had a turbulent relationship with his public and his editors.

## A lasting marriage

Thomas and Emma moved into Max Gate in June 1885, after more than ten years of married life. Although their relationship had cooled and Hardy's Christian faith had waned whilst Emma became increasingly devout, they remained together until her death in 1912. They shared a life and various interests, such as their beloved pets, long cycle rides and foreign holidays. When Emma died Hardy was inconsolable and the ensuing remorse and regret led him to write some of the greatest and most moving love poems in the English language.

Left Architectural drawing of Max Gate by Thomas Hardy

Above Max Gate
seen from the
garden

He did, however, marry again. Hardy had met Florence Dugdale, an admirer who also had literary aspirations, in 1904, possibly at a garden party, although she often gave different versions to different people of their first meeting. In 1905 Florence met Emma Hardy at the Lyceum Club in London, of which they were both members, and they too became friends. Emma invited Florence to Max Gate to help her with her work. Soon Florence began helping Hardy with research for *The Dynasts* and later with secretarial work. Their relationship deepened and two years after Emma's death, Florence, who was 39 years his junior, became Hardy's second wife and remained with him until his death in 1928.

# The house that Hardy built

**When Thomas and Emma moved to Max Gate in 1885, they were both in their forties. Large enough to accommodate a family, and later extended, Max Gate never had need of a nursery, but it was big enough to entertain wider family and friends and to receive some illustrious company.**

As an architect, Hardy had designed a variety of buildings, including houses. He designed Max Gate for his own use and it was built by the family firm. It occupied a remote and exposed site. While still renting Shire-Hall Place, Hardy began planting trees on the high windswept ridge and eventually there were several thousand, mostly beech trees and Austrian pines, providing privacy as well as shelter. A brick wall, nearly six feet high, was also built around the southern and eastern sides of the property.

Max Gate is modestly proportioned and clearly architect-designed. The original design was for a Victorian villa with two storeys and an attic. There were two reception rooms, two bedrooms and, the heart of the house, a study. But, like the cottage, Max Gate has been added to and extended. Hardy's fame and fortune grew with each novel published while he was there.

The grounds turned out to be rich in archaeological interest, being on the site of a Neolithic stone circle and a Romano-British cemetery. In more recent history it had been where the tollgate keeper, Henry Mack, lived and was consequently known as Mack's Gate by locals.

Above **The Porch**

Left **Max Gate stood in virtual isolation when it was built in 1885**

# The Entrance Hall

**Hardy gave much thought to light when designing and adapting his house. In the Entrance Hall internal windows above the main staircase cleverly 'borrow' light, illuminating a space that would otherwise have been far less inviting.**

The Entrance Hall received so many famous and talented individuals there is not the room to list them here. Here are quotations from just a few of the writers, who were among the Hardys' many guests.

'He seemed cheerful, his main dread being interviewers, American ladies, and the charabancs that whirr past while the conductor shouts "Ome of Thomas 'Ardy, novelist"'

E.M. Forster

'That man couldn't look out of a window without seeing something that had never been seen before.'

J.M. Barrie

'After tea we went into the garden, where he asked to see some of my poems… He said that he could sit down and write novels by a timetable, but that poetry always came to him by accident, which perhaps, was why he prized it more highly.'

Robert Graves

Left Light floods into the Entrance Hall through the stairwell windows

Far left Coat rack in the Entrance Hall

# The Dining Room

**This room saw some highly influential people sit down to dinner.**

Among the many distinguished visitors who dined at Max Gate were Edward, Prince of Wales, the poet W.B. Yeats, Rudyard Kipling, James Barrie (author of *Peter Pan*), and writer and aristocrat Lady Cynthia Asquith. Others were the sculptor Sir Hamo Thornycroft and his wife, Agatha. The latter is said to have been the inspiration for Tess; indeed, Hardy himself acknowledged this. The writer Edmund Gosse recalled meeting Hardy by chance in the National Gallery, and Hardy telling him that he was feeling more cheerful because he had just seen the 'most beautiful woman in England – her on whom I thought when I wrote Tess'. Hardy enjoyed discussing poetry with Hamo Thornycroft's nephew, Siegfried Sassoon. Another favourite was T.E. Lawrence, who lived nearby at Clouds Hill and asked Robert Graves for an introduction.

Above The Dining Room

## Original solutions

Most of the contents of Max Gate were auctioned, as directed in Florence Hardy's will, but this room does have a few original pieces, notably the removable bookcases, designed by Hardy. These were particularly admired by T.E. Lawrence, who wrote about them in his diary.

Another interesting aspect of Hardy's design in this room are the horizontal sash shutters on the windows. Hardy himself was quite a draw and there was a time when passers-by could come right up to the house, so to ensure some privacy he had this unusual but effective feature installed.

### Animals at dinner

Dinner was generally a formal occasion and the atmosphere and furnishings of this room reflect that purpose. However, formal apparently did not always mean conventional. A quite extraordinary dinner was reported by the poet Sir Henry Newbolt: 'I could hear and see Mrs [Emma] Hardy giving [W.B.] Yeats much curious information about two very fine cats, who sat right and left of her plate on the table itself... Yeats looked like an Eastern Magician overpowered by a Northern Witch – I too felt myself spellbound by the famous pair of Blue Eyes, which surpassed all that I had ever seen.' Years later, Lady Cynthia Asquith, dining at Max Gate along with the author J.M. Barrie, reported Wessex, the terrier Florence Hardy had brought with her to Max Gate, actually walking about on the table, hungrily watching the diners with clear resentment.

**Opposite** The window is partly obscured by a shutter, which Hardy had built for privacy

**Above** These removable bookcases were designed by Hardy; they are original to the house

# The Drawing Room

This room was also known as the Music Room. Music had been a key feature of Thomas's childhood and here Hardy played the violin while Emma accompanied him on the piano. Visitors, friends and family were frequently entertained in this room. During Florence's time Hardy's sisters came to visit often. Also in the later years, when some of Hardy's novels were adapted for the theatre, this is where the Hardy Players would plan their productions and rehearse. Actors from the 1925 London production of *Tess* came to give a performance in this room too, as Hardy had not felt able to go to the capital to see the play.

Tea was taken here at 4 o'clock every day. Thomas was at great pains to have this space for entertaining make the most of the available daylight. When the house was first built the main window, unusually large for a Victorian house, would have afforded uninterrupted views of the garden, Came Woods and the hills beyond.

## Personal touches
The overmantle above the fireplace, which pre-dates the house, was specially built to accommodate a Venetian-style mirror. The Delft tiles are original to the house and are said to have been collected by Hardy while on a cycling holiday in Holland.

## The conservatory
The extension to this room was built in 1895, but the conservatory was added after Hardy's marriage to Florence. The bench with cast-iron sides, the wrought-iron garden chair and the large urn are all original to the house. The conservatory leads on to the middle lawn, where garden parties, in which Emma Hardy delighted, were regularly held.

## A quick getaway
Across the lawn is a small door in the perimeter brick wall. This was Hardy's escape route when visitors proved too much. He was sometimes a reluctant host, perhaps considering it a necessary but not always enjoyable aspect of the work of a famous writer, which explains why some found him amiable and generous, while others were less impressed.

Right The Drawing Room

Left Hardy would escape through this gate when visitors became too much for him

## Shared passions

Although Hardy's marriage to Emma was subject to much strain, they retained some joint interests. They doted on their animals, possibly surrogates for the children they never had, and shared a love of the outdoors. Their courtship had after all begun on the cliff-tops of Cornwall and Hardy was a great walker. When Emma took up cycling at the age of 55 she shared her new-found passion with her husband. Her bicycle was green and named 'The Grasshopper'. She had a green velvet cycling suit and hat, which became a familiar sight in Dorchester and when she traded 'The Grasshopper' in for a blue bicycle, her outfit was changed to match.

# The Hardys' hired help

**Emma would have been brought up in a household with servants. Hardy's experience was different. His mother (who had been in domestic service herself), grandmother and sisters would all have been involved in running the household. Now that Hardy had the means – and a wife who would have insisted upon it – it is not at all surprising that the Hardys had hired help.**

In *The Hand of Ethelberta*, published in 1876, Hardy has some fun with the structures and strictures of Victorian society. The heroine, born to parents in service, has managed through education to escape her class and has made a name for herself as a poet. Left a widow, she shows remarkable energy and initiative in earning a living and providing work for her father, her numerous brothers and her sister, as servants in her household, while concealing their relationship to her from the rest of the world.

## Domestic arrangements

In 1909 there were three live-in servants at Max Gate: the housemaids, Jane and Daisy, and the housekeeper, Florence Griffin. The cook's position was filled by various women who lived nearby. Staff turnover was quite high at Max Gate as the Hardys had exacting standards.

The Kitchen and service rooms are at the back and there were bedrooms for servants in the attic. Originally all the water for the household had to be drawn daily by a hand pump from the well in the garden. There was no boiler, which meant that all water had to be heated in kettles and pans over the kitchen fire; the stoves and fires were designed to burn

Below Servants' bells at Max Gate

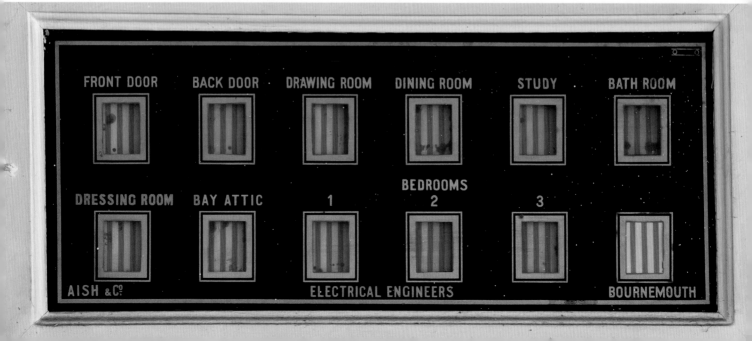

FRONT DOOR   BACK DOOR   DRAWING ROOM   DINING ROOM   STUDY   BATH ROOM

DRESSING ROOM   BAY ATTIC   BEDROOMS   1   2   3

AISH & Cº   ELECTRICAL ENGINEERS   BOURNEMOUTH

Above Detail of the black range installed in 1914 with Florence's arrival

Right The W.C.

either coal or peat. Dorchester gained an electricity supply in 1901, but Max Gate was not connected until 1924, so until that time lighting was provided by oil lamps and candles. In February 1921 Siegfried Sassoon wrote in his diary, 'Was it the author of *The Dynasts* who went up the dark stairs in front of you carrying a silver candlestick, and showed you, with a touch of pride, the new bathroom?'

## Kitchen

Part of the 1894–95 expansion of the house, the Kitchen still has its original dresser. When this extension was built, the small black range was probably moved from the old kitchen (later the Bicycle Room).

## Bathroom

The Bathroom, which you will see upstairs, was an addition insisted upon by Florence and she had it installed in 1920. It was supplied with hot running water, although Hardy preferred to bathe in a tin bath, filled by maids, in his bedroom. The deep cast-iron roll-top bath, with combined waste and overflow, possibly manufactured by Twyfords of Staffordshire, is from that time and there would have been a pedestal washbasin by the same manufacturer.

## W.C.

Modern conveniences in the 1880s included a flush lavatory but no plumbing; the water drawn by maids from the well in the garden would have been carried in jugs to fill a roof tank that fed taps and flushed the toilet. Later the system became slightly more mechanised with the arrival of a hand pump. Bertie Stephens, who was the gardener at Max Gate in the last years of Hardy's life, described how he had to pump it 200 times daily to fill the tank in the roof, twice a day if there were visitors.

Taking a leaf out of Reverend Henry Moule's book (see page 21), Hardy designed a system for re-using waste in the garden – the pump over the cesspit is still there today. He also re-used water that drained into a tank under the Kitchen.

# Hardy's Second Study

This was Hardy's interim study, after he turned his first into a bedroom in 1887. He reportedly found this room small and difficult to work in. Despite it being less than perfect for its purpose, this was the room in which Thomas penned *Tess of the d'Urbervilles* and *Jude the Obscure*, his final novel.

This room is much altered since the time it was used as Hardy's study; the window alcove was added in 1914 and the bookcases in the corridor were part of this room before the partition was put in to access the third and final study.

## The trouble with Tess

Tess is Thomas Hardy's best-known heroine, a potent literary figure, and it seems she had an enduring effect on her creator. In addition to Agatha Thornycroft, mentioned earlier, another likely inspiration for the character was a dairymaid, Augusta Way. Hardy encountered her when she was 18 years old and was greatly struck by her beauty. An interesting postscript to that story is that Augusta's daughter married a certain Arthur Bugler and their daughter, Gertrude Bugler, was cast as Tess, in a dramatisation of the novel performed by the Hardy Players. Hardy described Gertrude as 'the impersonator of Tess'.

Hardy loved beauty in all things and this included women. In 1883, two years after the publication of *Tess*, Thomas and Emma were in Dublin as the guests of the Lord-Lieutenant of Dublin, Lord Houghton, later the Marquess of Crewe. Here they met Lord Houghton's daughter, Florence Henniker, to whom Hardy was immediately and powerfully attracted. Florence was a novelist, the god-daughter of Florence Nightingale, and was married to Arthur Henniker, a professional soldier. Hardy rapidly cultivated a relationship with Florence and she was the subject of several poems (see, for example, 'At an Inn' and 'A Broken Appointment'). She was also an inspiration for Sue Bridehead in *Jude the Obscure*. Although

Above First page of *Tess of the d'Urbervilles*

romantic setting of the Larmer Tree Gardens, built and owned by the famous archaeologist General Augustus Lane Fox Pitt-Rivers. On the occasion of this visit, Hardy and Agnes were the lead couple in moonlit country dancing among the trees. This is recalled in the poem, 'Concerning Agnes', which Hardy wrote after her death in 1926. He also wrote in his autobiography that this was the last occasion on which he, so 'passionately fond of dancing … from earliest childhood', ever danced.

*Tess of the d'Urbervilles* upset many people with its direct challenges to accepted Victorian morality and the teachings of the Church. Incensed by one review in particular, Hardy wrote, 'How strange that one may write a book without knowing what one puts into it – or rather, the reader reads into it! Well, if this sort of thing continues no more novel writing for me. A man must be a fool to deliberately stand up to be shot at.' The novel caused controversy but it made Hardy one of the best-known authors of the day and brought him considerable financial gain. Such was the demand for *Tess,* once it was serialised in *The Graphic,* a popular magazine of the time, and then published in a three-volume edition in 1891, that a single-volume edition was published within a year.

Above Thomas Hardy in his second study, as featured in *Black & White* magazine

Below left Gertrude Bugler, the 'impersonator of Tess'

Below right Programme for a performance of *Tess of the d'Urbervilles* by the Hardy Players

Florence did not feel as strongly for Hardy as he did for her and made it clear that she would not break her marriage vows, they remained friends until her death in 1923.

Another beautiful, intelligent and literary woman to whom Hardy was attracted was Agnes Grove. He met her in 1885, in the

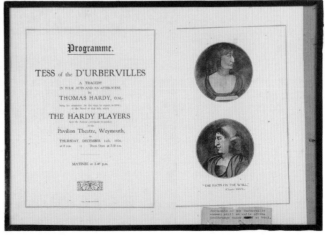

# The ideal study

**Thomas's fame and fortune continued to grow and following the success of *Tess of the d'Urbervilles* and *Jude the Obscure*, he could afford to expand Max Gate. In 1894–95 a new, larger kitchen and scullery were built, with Hardy's third study above, and two attic rooms for Emma's use.**

*Jude the Obscure* was certainly successful but the furore and negative reviews it provoked were considerable. One of the strongest objectors to this novel was Emma, who was deeply shocked by its subject matter and ideas. Alfred Sutro, a journalist and playwright who was visiting the Hardys in 1895, recalled Emma telling him that *Jude* was the first novel of Hardy's that he had published without letting her read the manuscript. Had she read it, she added firmly, 'it would not have been published, or at least, not without considerable emendations.' Following the reception of *Jude*, Hardy finally abandoned the novel form and, now financially secure, concentrated on his first love, poetry.

This room, his largest study, was the environment in which Hardy composed most of his enormous output of poetry. His first collection, *Wessex Poems*, was published when he was 58 and he went on to produce several more books of poems, as well as his epic verse drama, *The Dynasts*. One advantage of this room was its distance from the entrance to the house, which meant less disturbance from callers and domestic activities. Years later,

however, Hardy did permit the installation and imposition of a telephone, another one of Florence's modernisations. The number was Dorchester 43.

## A window on the world

Sensitive to the world about him, Hardy observed it in great detail in all weathers and through the changing seasons. Like an Impressionist painter, he would strive to capture the fleeting effects of light and use such effects to set the mood of particular scenes. So it's hardly surprising that the most striking feature of his favourite room are the large windows. These were designed without mullions and transoms at their centre, so that the view of the garden, with its changing patterns of light and shade, would be unobscured. Sitting at his desk by this window, Hardy would have enjoyed the morning sunlight on the garden and, at the end of the day, the reflected light on the trees.

## Study in detail

After Florence's death in 1937, the contents of Hardy's study – writing materials, bookcases containing reference books and many first editions, tables and chairs, and even the fireplace featuring Minton tiles by noted designer John Moyr Smith – were left to the Dorset County Museum in Dorchester. There the study has been reconstructed. There are some fascinating details, such as the calendar permanently set to the date Hardy met his first wife Emma – 7 March 1870; the pens, into the shafts of which he etched the names of the works written with them; the portraits hanging over the fireplace of individuals particularly important to him, including George Meredith, the man who gave him such valuable advice about his novel writing.

Left Hardy's third and final study

When the 1894–5 alterations were being planned, Emma asked Thomas to create her a space in which she could write, paint, read and sew in peace. While this was being achieved she took herself off to Calais for several weeks. The result of her request was these attic rooms, which she described as her 'sweet refuge and solace [where] not a sound scarcely penetrates hither'.

Emma started to use the rooms as a daytime retreat, but by 1899 she decided to move her bedroom up there. Hardy, always an assiduous worker, spent the greater part of each day in his study, to the end of his life. In these attic rooms Emma had her own space to pursue her varied interests. These included being an active supporter of women's suffrage. She wrote a letter to the journal, *Nation*, in 1908, arguing for women's participation in government and she also joined suffragette marches and attended rallies.

## The Old Affection

In the autumn of 1912 Emma was unwell and in pain with an undiagnosed condition. She was reluctant to see a doctor and even when she did, on 26 November, she apparently refused to let him examine her. At eight o'clock the following morning, her maid Dolly Gale was

Above Emma's Bedroom in the attic

terrified by the change she saw in Emma. Dolly alerted Hardy but by the time he arrived at his wife's bedside Emma was unconscious and minutes later she died. The doctor gave the cause of death as heart failure and impacted gallstones. She was buried three days later at St Michael's Church in Stinsford. Hardy had a wreath inscribed: 'From her Lonely Husband, with the Old Affection'.

## Poems of love and grief

Hardy had been devoting his time to poetry since 1895, but it is a widely held view that his finest poetry came with the outpouring of grief and remorse in the wake of Emma's death. In death, she proved his greatest inspiration. Just as their long-distance courtship, during which he had few opportunities to spend time with her, had inspired *A Pair of Blue Eyes*, this final separation sparked feelings of that love, renewed and recalled. Throughout the rest of his life his output of poetry was prolific and covered a wide range of subjects, but it continued to include poems which were honest and eloquent about their relationship.

**Above right** Emma was a talented watercolourist, as this painting of Blackmore Vale clearly shows

**Right** Emma in her later years

### Two Lips

*I kissed them in fancy when I came
Away in the morning glow:
I kissed them through the glass of her picture-frame:
She did not know.*

*I kissed them in love, in troth, in laughter,
When she knew all; long so!
That I should kiss them in a shroud thereafter
She did not know.*

# The Master Bedroom

The Master Bedroom was used by the master of the house, Hardy, firstly with Emma and then, after 1914, with his second wife, Florence. Although separate bedrooms for affluent married couples were not unusual in the Victorian period, there is no evidence that Hardy and Emma did not share this room, until 1899 when Emma began to use one of her attic rooms as a bedroom. Similarly, Hardy himself occupied a separate bedroom towards the end of his life. This was the room that had been his original study, on the other side of the connecting dressing room. (The dressing room is not currently open to the public.)

## A growing divide

The promise of the early romance between Hardy and Emma was not fulfilled in the reality of married life. As the years went by Hardy became increasingly respected as a great man of letters while Emma was less involved in his work. They were both fond of children and Hardy became a supportive uncle to Emma's niece and nephew. The fact that they remained childless would have strained their relationship. There is a poignant note in Hardy's autobiography when he has heard that their former servant is expecting a baby and writes, 'Yet never a sign of one is there for us.' Hardy's published and public avowals of the impossibility of a happy marriage and his questioning of religion, whilst Emma became increasingly devout, would have widened the divide between them.

Left **Florence and Thomas**

Right **Looking across the landing into Hardy's Bedroom**

Opposite **Hardy and his friend, the writer Edmund Gosse, in the garden at Max Gate**

# Hardy's First Study and Bedroom

**Here Hardy corrected the proofs of *The Mayor of Casterbridge* and wrote *The Woodlanders*. The former portrays a truly tragic character and was written while Hardy was living in the centre of Dorchester (Casterbridge). *The Woodlanders* is also a story of tragedy. It deals with issues of class, women and their roles, relationships and divorce, and it captures both the harshness and the beauty of rural life. After completing this book, Hardy took Emma for a six-week holiday in Italy.**

## No longer a study

Just a couple of years after moving into Max Gate, towards the end of 1887, Hardy turned his study into a bedroom, relocating the study to the small guest bedroom in the north-west corner of the house. When the writer Edmund Gosse came to stay in 1886 he occupied what Hardy described as 'only a bachelor's room'. However, his host informed him that by the following year Edmund and Mrs Gosse would both be able to stay, in 'a regulation spare-bedroom for married couples' i.e. this room, once it was no longer required as a study. Hardy may also have used it himself at times and he was certainly using it at the end of his life, as we know it was here that he died.

In 1914 Hardy married Florence Dugdale, 39 years his junior. She was a great admirer of this literary giant and had her own ambitions to be a writer. As his wife she continued to assist him with his work, which must have involved typing up much poetry professing his love for Emma.

It was not only a dead wife with whom Florence had to compete. Gertrude Bugler, the talented actress whom Hardy admired and who played the part of Tess in the Hardy Players' dramatisation of *Tess of the d'Urbervilles*, was invited to play the role in London, a life-changing opportunity for her. Florence believed that Hardy was so dangerously infatuated with Gertrude that she intervened, without her husband's knowledge, and persuaded the young woman to turn down the part.

Whatever the trials Florence experienced, she looked after Hardy to the end, nursing him with the help of her sister Eva, a trained nurse, in his final days. Florence was with him when he died in this room on 11 January 1928. His last meal that morning was his childhood favourite, bacon cooked on the fire. At dusk he asked Florence to read to him from Edward Fitzgerald's *The Rubaiyat of Omar Khayyam*, a work he greatly admired. Later that evening, following a heart attack, he died.

# The Garden

**When Hardy designed the garden he had no idea of the ancient history and stories that were later to be revealed under the ground of the plot he had purchased.**

He planted a forest of Austrian pines – 'I set every tree in my June time… And now they obscure the sky' ('At Day-Close in November') – but many were cut down by Florence in the interval between his death and hers nine years later. In *The Woodlanders* there is a scene in which Giles Winterborne and Marty South are planting trees and imagining their sighs as they are placed into their holes. Such a feeling for plants is not perhaps so unusual in woodsmen and Hardy himself had such an affinity with nature that he would talk to the trees and was careful not to 'hurt' his plants.

The trees repaid him in inspiration. Running between the east wall and a hedge is the Nut Walk. Weather and health permitting, Hardy would walk here every day. This was the 'alley of bending boughs' that features in his poem 'The Going', written soon after Emma's death and in which he momentarily imagines seeing her again:

*Why do you make me leave the house*
*And think for a breath it is you I see*
*At the end of the alley of bending boughs*
*Where so often at dusk you used to be*

Right **The garden today**

## Archaeology at Max Gate

This house was built on an ancient stone circle, older than Stonehenge and Avebury. One of the stones was found and was placed in the garden in Hardy's time. This features in the poem, 'The Shadow on the Stone', in which Hardy forlornly imagines the shadow as being cast by Emma as she gardens. A century later, during excavations prior to the construction of the Dorchester bypass, another 'sarsen' stone was found and also set in the Max Gate garden.

The excavation of the drive revealed Roman occupation and in particular two skeletons from a Romano-British cemetery. The first talk which Hardy gave in the Dorset County Museum, in 1884, was about the Romano-British finds on the Max Gate site.

## The Pet Cemetery

On the western side of the garden Hardy and Emma created a final resting place for their beloved pets and some of the headstones were carved by Hardy. As cosseted as they were, a number of these animals came to untimely ends, which must have been traumatic for their owners: the black retriever Moss was beaten to death by a passing tramp; their cats, Pella, Kitsey and Snow-dove, were all killed on the railway line.

Perhaps loved above all others was Wessex, Florence's terrier, who had a tendency to bite visitors. Hardy and both his wives were devoted to cats. Later occupants of Max Gate carried on the tradition of keeping cats and dogs and burying their pets here.

### An animal lover and defender

Hardy loved all animals and a large number of his poems are about animals and birds. However, his concern for them went much further. He was highly sensitive to the suffering of his fellow human beings and a logical extension of this was his reaction to cruelty against animals. He protested against the use of horses in battle in the Boer War, decried the mass slaughter of game birds on country estates, was an active supporter of the League for the Prohibition of Cruel Sports and wrote the poem 'Compassion' as an ode to the RSPCA on the occasion of its 100th anniversary in 1924.

Above left **Thomas and Florence with Wessex in 1914**

Left **Wessex's headstone**

# A Difficult Man to Know?

Left **Thomas Hardy in his mid-seventies**

Thomas Hardy was world-famous in his lifetime but remained quite a private and sometimes shy person. He deplored the injustices of society but sought acceptance by the establishment. This he certainly found. The eight pall-bearers at his funeral were James Barrie, John Galsworthy, Edmund Gosse, A.E. Housman, Rudyard Kipling and George Bernard Shaw, all representing the literary world; and the Prime Minister, Stanley Baldwin and the Leader of the Opposition, Ramsay MacDonald, representing Parliament.

## Remembering Hardy

Hardy was a great celebrity in his day. He received many honours, including the Order of Merit, five honorary university doctorates and the Gold Medal of the Royal Society of Literature, which was presented to him at Max Gate on his 72nd birthday by the poets W.B. Yeats and Henry Newbolt. He declined a knighthood, but was delighted to be granted the Freedom of Dorchester.

Now his admirers come from all corners of the world to visit his homes in Bockhampton and Dorchester. His works illuminate the fine detail and beauty found in nature, explore the complex motivations behind human behaviour and challenge accepted views about Victorian society and the institutions it held sacred. If the questions he asked made him unpopular in some quarters during his lifetime, nearly 90 years after his death his novels and poems still enthrall and move millions of readers. The poem 'Afterwards' sums up how he would have liked to be remembered.

## Afterwards

*When the Present has latched its postern behind my tremulous stay,*
    *And the May month flaps its glad green leaves like wings,*
*Delicate-filmed as new-spun silk, will the neighbours say,*
    *'He was a man who used to notice such things'?*

*If it be in the dusk when, like an eyelid's soundless blink,*
    *The dew-fall hawk comes crossing the shades to alight*
*Upon the wind-warped upland thorn, a gazer may think,*
    *'To him this must have been a familiar sight.'*

*If I pass during some nocturnal blackness, mothy and warm,*
    *When the hedgehog travels furtively over the lawn,*
*One may say, 'He strove that such innocent creatures should come to no harm,*
    *But he could do little for them; and now he is gone.'*

*If, when hearing that I have been stilled at last, they stand at the door,*
    *Watching the full-starred heavens that winter sees,*
*Will this thought rise on those who will meet my face no more,*
    *'He was one who had an eye for such mysteries'?*

*And will any say when my bell of quittance is heard in the gloom,*
    *And a crossing breeze cuts a pause in its outrollings,*
*Till they rise again, as they were a new bell's boom,*
    *'He hears it not now, but used to notice such things'?*

Above Front page of the *Daily Mirror*, 17 January 1928. Hardy's funeral was held at Westminster Abbey on 16 January, but a burial was held at Stinsford Church where his heart was interred next to Emma. His ashes, meanwhile, are in the Abbey's famous Poets' Corner

Left Hardy's burial at Stinsford Church

# Very different homes

Hardy's Cottage and Max Gate say a great deal about the life of Thomas Hardy and can enhance our appreciation of this great writer. We hope your experience of them has revealed more about the man and inspired you to read further.

### At Hardy's Cottage
*Desperate Remedies* (1871)
*Under the Greenwood Tree* (1872)
*A Pair of Blue Eyes* (1873)
*Far from the Madding Crowd* (1874)

### Other Locations – London and Dorset
*The Hand of Ethelberta* (1876)
*The Return of the Native* (1878)
*The Trumpet-Major* (1880)
*A Laodicean* (1881)
*Two on a Tower* (1882)

### At Max Gate
*The Mayor of Casterbridge* (1886)
*The Woodlanders* (1887)
*Wessex Tales* (1888)
*Tess of the d'Urbervilles* (1891)
*A Group of Noble Dames* (1891)
*Life's Little Ironies* (1894)
*Jude the Obscure* (1895)
*The Well-Beloved* (1897)
*Wessex Poems* (1898)
*Poems of the Past and the Present* (1902)
*Time's Laughingstocks* (1909)
*The Dynasts* (1910)
*Satires of Circumstance* (1914)
*Moments of Vision* (1917)
*Late Lyrics and Earlier* (1922)
*Human Shows* (1925)
*Winter Words* (1928)

Left Hardy's Cottage and Max Gate as they were in Hardy's time